MOOSE COUNTRY

Moose Country

SAGA OF THE WOODLAND MOOSE

BY MICHAEL W.P. RUNTZ

FOREWORD BY

DR. A.B. BUBENIK

Published in the United States of America by NorthWord Press, Inc.

For a free catalogue describing NorthWord's line of nature books and gifts, call 1-800-336-5666 or write to NorthWord Press, Inc., Box 1360, Minocqua, WI 54548.

Printed in Hong Kong.

Contents

To the memory of Bud Levy,
who during my formative years helped to fan a spark of interest in
the natural world into a flame of passion

Acknowledgments

THE AUTHOR IS INDEBTED to the many people who assisted in the production of this book. I am especially grateful to Dan Strickland and Peter Smith, both of the Ontario Ministry of Natural Resources, for introducing me to the magic of "moosing," for their companionship and for the valued knowledge they imparted during many exciting excursions. Other Natural Resources personnel, Ron Tozer and Mike Wilton in particular, offered advice and logistics. Thanks also to Marc Denis for his assistance in locating rutting pits and to Peter Hessel for tracking down the Algonkian origin of the moose's name. In particular, Dr. A. (Tony) B. Bubenik deserves special credit, not only for his invaluable advice and comments but also for providing the foreword to this manuscript and for producing the range map. A special thanks is owed to my wife, Heather, and son, Harrison, for their support during my frequent disappearances into moose country.

Foreword

BY ITS BODY PROPORTIONS, antlers' shape and size, and demeanor, the moose is the mighty symbol of the boreal and subarctic zones of the entire northern hemisphere. To describe moose country, an immense area of different habitats, is not easy. However, in simplified form, moose country is the variously dense mixed forest, called taiga or "northern bush," on the one hand; on the other hand, it is the open "forest-tundra," where conifers, ten to fourteen feet (three to four metres) high, dwarf-birch, alder and willows are scattered, mostly around lakes, bogs and streams.

The climate differs from zone to zone, and moose prefer only those zones where the average summer temperature does not much exceed sixty degrees Fahrenheit (15 degrees Celsius). Wind chill or lake abundance help the moose to stay cool in the coastal and relatively humid zones, as well as in the much drier interior. Thus, in evolutionary terms, the moose has had to adapt both to humid and dry climates, and to dense and open habitats.

By looking at the wide geographic range shown on the map on the next two pages, it seems logical to conclude that many subspecies of moose might have evolved. Indeed, officially, these subspecies number seven or eight. However, the differences among the subspecies need not concern the reader. What is important is that the moose as we know it evolved in central or western Europe about six hundred thousand years ago. From there moose migrated up to the most eastern tip of Siberia, where they were forced to stop; then, about two hundred and fifty thousand to one hundred thousand years ago, the sea level of the Bering Strait dropped so much that a passage over solid land to Alaska was possible.

This first migratory wave arrived probably from the humid and dense taiga of the Far East, where the dark-colored moose with small body size and narrower spread of antlers still lives. It seems likely the dry climate and open habitat of Alaska's forest-tundra did

Moose are the largest inhabitants of the northern forest.

The moose inhabits much of the boreal and subarctic regions of the world. Algonquin Provincial Park, Ontario,
one of the finest moose viewing areas, is highlighted.

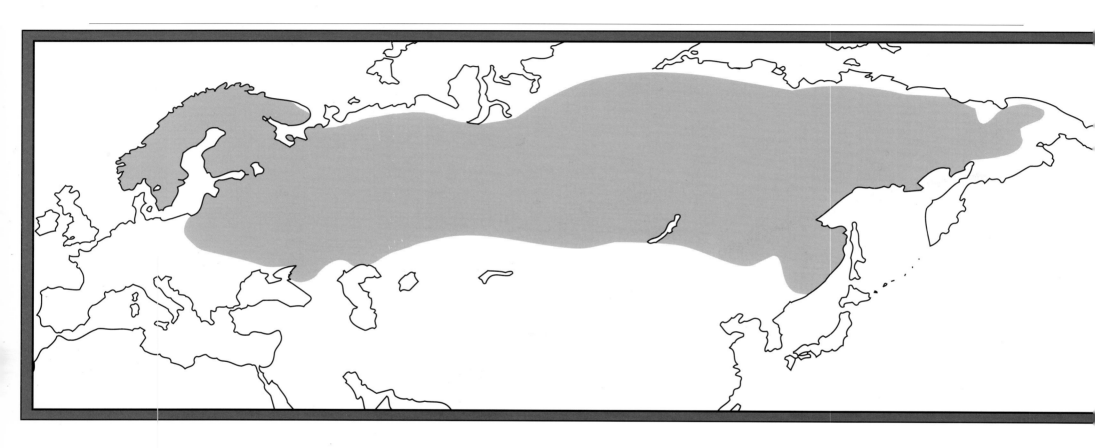

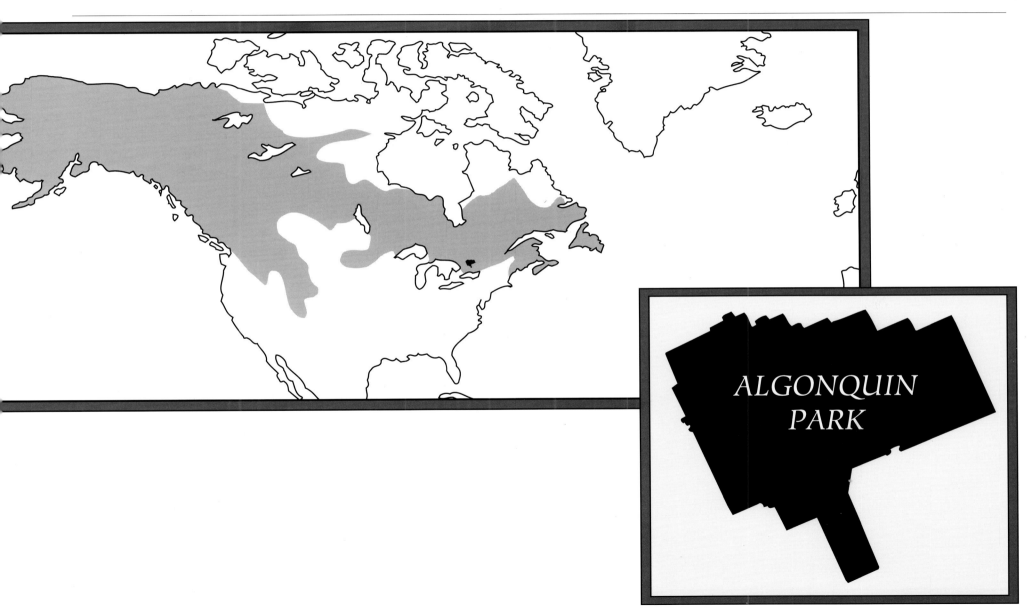

ALGONQUIN
PARK

not suit them. This might well be the reason for their push southward, toward the Great Lakes and forested coasts, before the ice shield of the Wisconsin Period developed a massive barrier from the Pacific to Atlantic oceans, about forty thousand years ago.

At about that time, the sea level in the Bering Strait dropped again, making it possible for the moose of the northern forest-tundra of Siberia to invade Alaska. Due to the Wisconsin ice shield, these moose could not and — as present distribution corroborates — would not move into the taiga. Because they had evolved in open habitat with very dry climate, the wet and dense taiga proved unsuitable. In the forest-tundra they also evolved a larger body size, pale coloration, wide antler spread and the harem-breeding strategy. In North America, these populations are classified as the giant moose, *Alces alces gigas*.

The moose of the North American taiga belt are classified as *Alces a. americana*, *Alces a. andersoni* and *Alces a. shirasi*, although such classification does not appear to be definitive. It is easier to lump all these subspecies under the general term of "woodland moose." By doing so, we effectively reduce moose country substantially. To examine the life of the woodland moose in general, we can look at one small part of the moose's range, in Algonquin Provincial Park in Ontario, Canada (see the insert on the map).

THAT MIKE ASKED ME to write this foreword could be viewed as either destiny or pure chance. Our common interest lies not only in our sharing an admiration for moose. One also can point to behavioral characteristics common to Mike, me and the moose: individualistic by nature, we elect to stay with our peers only if it suits our mood or attitude; and we all met in Algonquin Provincial Park.

For myself and Mike, to understand moose means to stay with moose year-round and become fluent in moose language. In my case, the interest in moose took more of an academic bent. A behavioral physiologist by profession and a scholar who has devoted his life to studying antler development from all possible aspects, I was also spurred by a need to discover why moose have evolved antlers of such great size and peculiar shape.

To keep this story brief, I was able to provide evidence that the antlers of large deer are organs of paramount social importance: they did not evolve as weapons for fighting and incapacitating. Antlers are primarily indicators of age and fitness, that is, of status or rank, visually assessed by females when selecting a mate. The antlered head of a bull moose is the only center of visual attention for both sexes. Because of their importance as a visual stimulant, a bipedal man with an antlered head is as readily accepted as any quadrupedal one, despite the presence of human scent. Ergo, I was able to study communication among moose by wearing an antlered dummy moose head.

A part of my studies was conducted in Algonquin Provincial Park, where the opportunity to admire Mike's color slides initially presented itself. I became impressed by his knowledge of moose behavior and keen interest in my studies. It was a distinct pleasure to be able to enlarge on Mike's own knowledge of moose and direct his attention to some important event of moose life, worthy of being photographed.

Mike's *Moose Country: Saga of the Woodland Moose* is, to my knowledge, the most fascinating photographic documentation of moose in the taiga habitat. I firmly believe readers will share this view.

IN A NATURAL SETTING, predators such as wolf or bear tend to have a positive effect on moose populations by culling out less able animals. Hunting, as with other beneficial predation, must go along with the needs of the moose, not those of the hunter. We must accept that we humans are more a part of the world of moose than vice versa. In this respect, current regulations for moose hunting are far removed from the role the hunter should play in moose ecology. The moose of Algonquin Provincial Park are fortunate not to have been exposed to the hunter's passion. (But this is another story.) I only hope Mike's book will awaken the interest of hunters and nonhunters alike, and help to change man's attitude toward moose hunting.

The pictures and commentary should contribute to a better understanding of these giants and their needs. Should this book achieve such a goal, it will not only be a great success for the author and publisher but also for the moose, the mighty monarch of the taiga.

Dr. A. (Tony) B. Bubenik

Preface

FIRST ENCOUNTERS

IT WAS A BITTERLY COLD MORNING one late September when I was first introduced to "moosing." Dan Strickland and Peter Smith, both with the Ontario Ministry of Natural Resources, had invited me to accompany them on one of their excursions to view moose during the rut in Algonquin Provincial Park. We set off into the darkness of the predawn, rumbling down a rugged back road. As we slowly drove by openings in the young forest of poplar and birch, our eyes anxiously scanned for the looming form of a moose. Suddenly, Peter's whisper broke the silence: "There's one — over on the left." The truck ground to a halt, and with the switching off of the headlights the darkness quickly swallowed us. When my eyes finally adjusted to the dim of the early morn, I could only discern the pale trunks of poplars perforating the gloom.

Peter slowly raised a worn birch-bark horn to his mouth and, after filling his lungs with the chilling night air, masterfully moaned out a penetrating nasal bawl. As the call reverberated through the trees, my ears strained to hear a response. Hearts leapt when a nearby ruffed grouse exploded into flight. Again, Peter raised the horn and called. This time the crack of wood under a heavy foot revealed the presence of a large animal. My heart began to pound wildly when suddenly a massive head adorned by an intimidating rack of bone appeared through the trees, a mere fifty feet (fifteen metres) away! The giant calmly stood there, staring intently our way. Dan began to thrash nearby shrubbery with a small set of antlers that previously had been resting over his shoulder. In immediate response, the bull lowered his mighty head and began to rock his antlers to and fro, whipping a small shrub into submission.

The sight of this monstrous beast performing an ageless ritual, seemingly oblivious to our presence, held me totally spellbound. This exhilarating experience was to be repeated countless times in the years following, as "moosing" became an integral part of my fall agenda.

Although during the remainder of the year moose may appear to be rather uninteresting, on closer scrutiny they portray a most complex life history, one profoundly structured and rich with astounding associations. This book is an attempt to capture and illustrate both the resplendence and the complexity of one of the largest and most amazing members of the wild, the moose of the northern woodlands.

Few animals present a stronger visual impact than does the moose.

CHAPTER ONE

Twig Eater

THE DISTURBED RUSTLING of leaves and the sharp snapping of twigs herald the approach of a formidable creature. Finally, through the vegetation an endless lanky leg protrudes, slowly followed by another. Towering above, the massive head of the great beast casually surveys the surrounding land. Its disproportionately elongated snout is raised, and the huge nostrils flare as the air is checked for the scent of unseen danger. Satisfied all is well, it saunters into the forest opening. Standing six feet (two metres) high at the shoulder and weighing over one thousand pounds (four hundred and fifty kilograms), this giant commands respect. Its long neck stretches, and with a quiet snap it rips the tender tips off nearby shrubs.

The Algonkian Indians had an appropriate name for this magnificent animal. Their word — "mons" or "moz" (depending on the dialect) — has been adopted into the English language as "moose." Although the word we currently use offers scant information about the animal, "twig eater" — a loose translation of the Algonkian term — provides an apt description of its diet.

North Americans refer to this animal as the moose; however, throughout continental Europe, it has often been known as the "elk." The scientific name, *Alces alces*, also translates into British English as "elk." For North Americans this has been a source of confusion, as the name "elk" is also given to another member of the deer family, the wapiti (*Cervus canadensis*). Unfortunately, the common names of many living things differ from region to region, from country to country. On the other hand, the scientific names, albeit frequently awkward to articulate, are universal in their usage and eliminate the confusion generated by the more familiar appellations.

As the Algonkians so astutely noted, moose are browsers, depending on plants for their nutrition. The largest members of the deer family (Cervidae), their vora-

At first glance it appears that the overhanging snout is a barrier to food. However, the lips are highly flexible and with them pulled back out of the way, the twigs are snipped off with the lower incisors.

cious appetites match their tremendous size. Since bulls may weigh over one thousand pounds (four hundred and fifty kilograms) and cows average only about two hundred pounds (ninety kilograms) less, a large amount of food, up to fifty pounds (twenty-three kilograms) or more per day, is required to fuel their energy requirements. Although moose lack teeth in the front of the upper jaw, they have little trouble dealing with the woody plant material that constitutes much of their diet. They feed on fresh leaves by browsing and may even pull a shoot sideways through their mouth, frequently stripping off up to two feet (one-half metre) of vegetation with the aid of the tough, thick tongue and lips. They also browse the tips of twigs, particularly the most recent growth. Regardless of how it is attained, the plant material is thoroughly crushed between twelve sets of broad, flattened teeth at the rear of the mouth, six pairs of molars and six pairs of premolars.

Once the partly ground food is swallowed, it enters the first of four stomach compartments, where bacteria begin to digest the material, breaking down the tough cellulose. Later, partly digested food in the form of a cud is regurgitated into the mouth for further, more leisurely mastication and more complete physical breakdown. Animals that recycle their food in this fashion are known as ruminants. Moose generally chew their cuds while comfortably lying down. When the cud is swallowed, further digestion takes place in the more distant stomach chambers.

Although many different plants are eaten by moose, the type consumed depends on the availability, both geographically and seasonally. In general, preferred trees and shrubs include willows (*Salix*), trembling aspen (*Populus tremuloides*), red-osier dogwood (*Cornus stolonifera*), red maple (*Acer rubrum*), striped maple (*Acer pennsylvanicum*), white birch (*Betula papyrifera*), beaked hazelnut (*Corylus rostrata*), pin cherry (*Prunus pennsylvanica*) and, primarily in winter, balsam fir (*Abies balsamea*). Aquatic plants, particularly water shield (*Brasenia schreberi*), yellow

Right: With its lanky legs, pendulous snout, dangling bell, oversized ears and, in the case of the bull, majestic antlers, the moose presents an easy form to recognize.
Below: Because a large part of its diet consists of woody material, the Algonkian Indians named this great beast "twig eater."

Through the season, a variety of plants are consumed. Balsam fir is an important winter food.

pond lily (*Nuphar* sp.) and pondweed (*Potamogeton* sp.), constitute a preferred and important part of the moose's diet in summer.

The thought of scrutinizing moose droppings may not be palatable to some. However, a closer look at the shape and texture of these waste products reveals the type of food eaten. The lush aquatic plants and moist, green leaves consumed in summer result in large, pie-shaped droppings that resemble those of domestic cows. Browse composed of the tougher, woody twigs of spring and fall ends up as large, moist, pellet-shaped deposits. And the dry winter diet, which also includes the evergreen needles of coniferous trees, produces pellet-shaped droppings with the texture of sawdust. The latter are the items occasionally varnished and sold commercially as earrings or key-ring bobs.

For such a large animal, the moose has an amazing ability to slip silently through dense forests, plough through deep snow, swim across crystal lakes and plod over quaking bogs. Long, powerful legs afford the necessary elevation for traversing both smothering blankets of snow and bottomless muskeg. The long legs also provide for a long stride, enabling the moose to achieve speeds of twenty-five miles (forty kilometres) per hour, even reportedly up to thirty-five miles (fifty-five kilometres) per hour. The distinctive foot of a moose, consisting of two large cloven toes that can spread apart and two smaller toes that appear as horny "dew claws" on the back of the legs, presents a wide surface that helps support the animal on soft terrain. The dew claws may also serve to help support the moose as it travels across unstable surfaces.

With its towering legs, elongated snout, oversized ears and, in certain seasons, a massive rack of antlers on the bull, the moose is an easy form to recognize. Although some body parts may be exaggerated in size, the same cannot be said of the diminutive tail, almost an embarrassment for such a large animal. Another fea-

Moose can also feed on leaves by pulling a branch sideways through the mouth, using the thick, tough tongue and lips to strip the leaves from the shoot.

Northern waterways are an important feature of moose country.

ture that sets the moose apart from other animals is the bizarre flap of skin that dangles from its chin. The purpose of this bell, or dewlap, has been the source of much conjecture. The bell is larger on bulls, and its shape changes with age, suggesting a possible function as a visual status symbol. Perhaps more important, the bell serves as a retainer for saliva that contains secretions known as sex pheromones, volatile chemical compounds that play important roles as sexual attractants and potent stimulators of sexual behavior during the breeding season, the rut.

Since the moose lives in an environment where visibility is often reduced by dense forest cover, senses other than sight must be keenly developed. With acute hearing and discriminating powers of smell, the moose perceives its environment in a fashion that we, with our blunted senses, have difficulty interpreting.

The ears of a moose are large and highly mobile, and their elongated cup shape serves to draw in and magnify a distant sound. As a moose feeds, the ears continuously survey the surrounding environment, detecting even the slightest rustle that might reveal an approaching predator. When a perturbing sound is discerned, the moose quickly swings its head in the direction of that sound, ears pricked up and pointing directly ahead. The nose and eyes also search for additional information as to the intruder's identity. A fascinating aspect of hearing in bulls is that their antlers may function as parabolic dishes, pulling in sounds from their surroundings. Thus, a bull can direct his ears towards the bony structures and be able not only to detect noises from a larger area but also, perhaps, to hear them in an amplified state.

Unquestionably, the moose has an incredibly keen sense of smell. The disproportionately long snout contains a vast number of nerve endings, sensitive to even the faintest of odors. In addition, a specialized center for smell analysis, the

Below: Moose are equally at home in water as they are on land. Excellent swimmers, moose can cross small bodies of water with relative ease.

During the summer, beaver ponds are frequently visited. These sites not only reward moose with feasts of succulent water plants but also may provide a cool watery escape both from hordes of biting flies and extreme heat.

Right: Moose country encompasses bog and stream, pond and forest.

Below: A moose foot consists of four toes: two large cloven ones, which offer support on soft surfaces; and two smaller horny dew claws on the rear, which possibly help to support the animal on unstable surfaces.

Right: In one set of tracks the animal was walking, and the dew claws do not leave an impression. In another, the deeper tracks complete with dew claw imprints reveal that the animal passed over the sand in a great hurry.

vomeronasal or Jacobson's organ, exists in the roof of the mouth. This complex center is vitally important in the discrimination of the sex pheromones, which are readily airborne and frequently carried in the urine of both sexes.

Due to our inability to view the world through the eyes of a moose, we have often interpreted its vision as being poor and of minor consequence. No doubt, some aspects of a moose's vision differ considerably from ours. Oval pupils provide a restricted vertical field of view in comparison to what we see. With the eyes placed more on the sides of the head, the moose achieves a very wide horizontal field of view but, unlike our vision, with little capacity for stereoscopic discrimination. However, the one major advantage moose have over us is that their eyes are highly mobile. They can be independently and easily directed to the front or to the rear. A moose can be standing, facing away from a person, but by merely rotating the eyes towards its backside, it can literally look behind itself to see the intruder without turning its head!

Perhaps the main difference between the vision of moose and humans is the superior ability of moose to see in low light conditions. Quite active at night, moose have adaptations for seeing at this time. As in other nocturnal animals, the moose has a special layer of cells, the tapetum lucidum, behind the retina. This layer acts as a reflector, recycling inside the eye light that would normally be wasted. Also, the abundance of rods in the eye allows for increased discrimination of contrasts in dimly lit situations. Thus, while the eyesight of moose has frequently been discredited, under certain conditions it is far superior to ours.

The moose not only imparts a powerful visual impact but also exhibits a fascinating, complicated life history. It inhabits a world of contrast, slipping through dense forests and traversing quaking bogs, suffering sweltering heat and surviving chilling cold. It shuns no time of day, being active in the deep darkness of night, as well as in the blinding brilliance of day. From the time spring bouquets color the forest floors, to the time suffocating snows dominate the land, appearances, as well as behaviors, change. The world of the moose is rich with seemingly bizarre relationships and elegant, ritualized responses. Once exposed to this realm of mystery and complexity, one's imagination is forever captured. And once held by its power, one is compelled to return, time and time again, to discover and explore further the fascinating secrets of moose country.

Below: Moose have acutely refined senses of hearing and smell. Although perhaps not as developed as the other senses, the eyesight of moose is by no means unimportant. Not only is their night vision far superior to ours but also their eyes are independently mobile, allowing moose to even see directly behind them.
Right: The ears of a moose are highly moveable, and are directed quickly towards a disturbing sound.

CHAPTER TWO

Beginnings

THE REVITALIZING WARMTH of the spring sun incites a profound change in northern landscapes. Almost overnight, vivid mosaics of spring flowers carpet the formerly barren forest floor. Overhead, buds burst open, sending forth regiments of unfurling leaves to capture the life-giving light. The air reverberates with song as scores of vibrant birds return to proclaim territories and attract desiring mates.

Spring is the season of birth for many animals, including the moose. By early May, last year's offspring, a close companion of its mother throughout the long, cold winter, is now considered an unwanted intruder and is driven off by the cow as she seeks solitude in which to bring forth the next generation. The youngster must be tremendously confused when its dam, formerly its source of life and nourishment, its consoler in times of stress and its protector in the face of danger, suddenly rejects it.

Bewildered by this reversal in attitude, the calf attempts to reunite with its mother, only to be rebutted repeatedly. Ultimately, the rejection is accepted, and the yearling must face the dangers of its world alone. It may for a time drift around the periphery of the cow's calving ground in the vain hope that she will discard her aggressiveness and once again tolerate its presence. Or the yearling may wander off, seeking a life completely on its own.

Why does the cow, after a year of intimate contact with her offspring, now try to drive it away when birthing time is near? Perhaps the extra attention drawn to a birth site by the yearling could prove fatal for the newborn calf. Wolves and, in particular, bears are known to feed on moose calves; therefore, for calf survival, the less activity around a birth site the better. For that reason, pregnant cows seek out sites where the chances are reduced of a predator surprising her and her newborn. Islands, surrounded by a chilling barrier of water, often offer the safest refuge, and peninsulas may also be favored.

The thick, plush coat of winter, vitally important in keeping the animals warm in sub-zero temperatures, is no longer needed as the warmth of spring returns. As their coats are shed, this cow and her last year's calf display the shabby appearance typical of moose in this season.

Enriched with the sodium that was absent from this animal's diet throughout the previous winter, the soft muck in roadside ditches is eagerly eaten.

Generally by mid- to late May, the cows arrive at their birth areas. If an island is chosen, the cow must swim through frigid waters. Whatever site is eventually chosen, the cow often selects the highest point of elevation on which to bring forth the new generation. By being elevated, the scent of approaching danger may be more quickly detected; also, the avenue of escape will be downhill in any direction, allowing for a faster retreat, often into the safety of water.

After eight months of imprisonment inside the maternal womb, the young are brought into the world among the leafy litter on the forest floor. A single calf might be the norm, but in regions where winter food is plentiful and population and parasite stresses are low, twins may prevail. In spring calf surveys in Algonquin Provincial Park, the twinning rate of cows was seen to fluctuate greatly over the years: in 1982, eighty percent of the cows had twins; in 1990, only seven percent were this productive. In Algonquin, the moose population increased rapidly through the 1970s and early 1980s. With an abundant supply of food and a low density of moose, there was plenty of room for a growing population, and twins dominated. By the mid-1980s, with the moose density well above one per square mile (two and a half square kilometres), the carrying capacity of the park — the maximum population that the park can safely support — was probably reached. With reduced availability of food and with increasing population and parasite stresses, single calves became the norm — as they are through much of the moose's range. In some instances, twins may predominate; rarely will triplets be born. In the latter case, generally one of the young is considerably smaller, with little chance for long-term survival.

Moose calves at birth appear rather ungainly. Their long, spindly legs seem ill-equipped for supporting the twenty-five to thirty-five pounds (eleven to fifteen kilograms) that the young animals weigh. Yet, only a matter of days pass before they are

Molt usually begins in the shoulder and upper-back region.

are able to run and swim with some proficiency. Although their legs and ears may appear oversized, the snout seems far more in proportion to the rest of the body than does that of the adult. Unlike the dark coloration of the mother, the young calves possess a light, sandy-colored pelage. The paleness of the fur accentuates the darkness of the eye and muzzle regions, rendering a forlorn expression to the calves.

Due to the almost constant bedding down of the cow and calf, the birth site soon acquires a worn, almost manicured appearance. Newly born moose calves depend entirely on the mother for both protection and food. Usually for the first few weeks of life, the cow's milk provides its only nourishment. This life-sustaining fluid is more than twice as concentrated as the milk of a domestic cow, and approximately one-half gallon (two litres) is needed daily to support the calf during the first month of life. Newborn calves are not capable of digesting foliage, for their gut lacks the essential bacteria needed to digest the plant material. However, a young calf receives the bacteria from its mother's saliva either directly through oral transfer or indirectly by ingesting it while nibbling on foliage on which the cow has previously browsed. As well, the newborn can obtain the bacteria by picking up in its mouth the droppings of either its mother or another moose. Eventually, a bacterial fauna will develop in the calf's gut, a fauna that enables it to digest the tough cellulose of plants, which will sustain it in later weeks. As summer progresses, browse becomes increasingly more important as the source of nutrition, and the calves are usually completely weaned by the onset of the breeding season in mid-September.

Young moose calves and their mothers are seldom far apart. If separated for even a short period of time, the high-pitched bleating of the calf and the guttural grunts of the cow soon serve to unite the pair. Constant licking of the calf and nose-nuzzling seems to reassure both the cow and calf that all is well; it could also serve to maintain and strengthen the bond between mother and infant. Usually, the animals

Cows seek out secluded sites, often near the safety of water, as the time of birth approaches. Islands are frequently chosen, for they not only offer many avenues of escape but also usually do not harbour bears, perhaps the main threat to newly born calves.

The highest elevation of the site is often chosen as the actual birthplace. Due to the constant bedding down of the cow and the newborn calf, the site acquires a worn appearance.

*Once inseparable, a cow now turns against her
yearling offspring and aggressively drives it away
when the time for the birth of a new generation nears.*

will try to flee from danger, but if the calf is too young to escape or is somehow physically impeded, the cow may charge whatever is threatening. If the threat persists, the cow will defend the calf by flailing with her front legs.

I will never forget the first time, one day in early June, I was charged by a cow tending her young calf. I had happened upon the pair among some pine trees bordering a logging road. As I slowly approached, the cow started to move away. The calf, which had been lying down, struggled to its feet and bleated rather pathetically. Immediately, the cow swung around and ran with incredible speed straight at me. My heart rate quickening, I fled out of the woods and back to the truck. The cow followed me until I was inside, then crossed to the far side of the road, calling to the calf with short grunts. When the cow was safely out of sight, I cautiously returned to the calf to examine it. As it struggled once more to its feet and tried to flee, I was able to discern that it had a broken hind leg — hence its inability to escape and hence the aggressiveness of the cow. Not wishing to disturb it further, I quickly left the scene. Undoubtedly, the calf would have had a very short life expectancy with a disability of that nature.

For many people, spring is the most opportune time for viewing moose. Moose are frequently seen along northern roadsides, down in the ditches drinking water and eating mud. This at first may seem to be rather eccentric behavior; yet, in terms of moose biology, it is rather justifiable. During the long winter months, when the diet of the moose consists mainly of the twigs and needles of trees, sodium, an essential element for life processes, is in low supply. In many northern areas, salt in the form of sodium chloride is employed as a means of keeping winter snows off the roads. This salt tends to become concentrated in roadside ditches due to the dual action of highway ploughs and spring run-off. Hence, moose that wander along the roadsides might find a readily available supply of sodium.

Calves are considerably paler in color and have a much shorter snout than the adults.

Left: At first sign of danger, a cow and her calf head for the safety of the water.
Below: A calf eagerly nurses while the cow closely watches for danger.

In some parts of their range, moose acquire sodium from certain water plants. In other regions, moose locate sodium and other minerals in the soil at sites known as mineral licks, where they lick or actually eat the earth. In so doing, moose obtain the vital sodium, as well as other elements. Although there have been conflicting opinions as to the exact type of nutrient derived at licks, there is convincing evidence that sodium is the primary attractant, necessary not only for moose but also for other ungulates (hoofed animals). However, sodium may not be present at all licks. In western North America, magnesium appears to be the main element derived from licks.

Why the necessity to replenish sodium (or magnesium) reserves? Plant tissue is generally low in sodium yet rich in potassium. Mammals must maintain relatively equal levels of both these elements, and ingesting high levels of potassium could result in internal physiological imbalances. Thus, moose and other ruminants must not only load up with sodium at certain times of the year, primarily spring and to a lesser degree autumn, but also recycle it so efficiently that they only need to saturate themselves with this element at most twice a year.

When a bull moose in his prime is viewed in the autumn, his massive antlers intimate power and supremacy. If the same animal was seen during the previous spring, it might have been difficult to accept that those great structures could arise from such humble beginnings. Unlike horns, a label many people erroneously apply to the bony structures of bull moose and other members of the deer family, antlers are deciduous in nature. The antlers of moose are similar to the leaves of hardwood trees in that they are discarded at the end of each year and replaced anew the following spring and summer. Often as early as late March, the developing antlers appear as swellings on the sides of the head, growing atop their perennial remnants known as pedicles. Pedicles are bony stalks that project upwards from the frontal bones of the skull. While they are growing, the antlers are covered in a distinctive skin that appears furry and soft. This special skin is equipped with a very dense pattern of sensitive nerves and many sebaceous glands. The plush, soft appearance due to the abundant short hairs growing perpendicular to the skin gives rise to its appropriate name of velvet. Underneath the velvet, arteries feed nourishment to the growing bone and veins collect the blood penetrating to the bone surface from the antler core. The sensitivity of the velvet is the reason for bulls avoiding contact and possible injury to the antlers during the first two-thirds of the growing period, when the antler material is soft and fragile. Only during the last trimester of the growth period, as the antlers achieve their magnificent optimum, does the dynamic mineralization occur, not only transforming the soft material into solid bone but also resulting in the death of the velvet.

Although moose may be rather easily observed in the spring, they are usually not at their photogenic best. The luxurious winter coat, once so vitally important in fending off winter's chill, is now no longer needed and is being shed at this time. The result is a very shabby appearance, quite different from that provided by either the lavish coat of winter or the sleek pelage of mid-summer. Molting, which begins about the shoulders of the front legs and the upper back region, creates a patchy, unsightly appearance. Furthermore, the bulls at this time of year sport only a mere suggestion of the majestic antler rack that will later develop. For these reasons, those who desire a breathtaking photograph of the lord of the land might consider delaying their photographic endeavors to a later season.

Right: Frequent exchanges of nuzzling and licking seem to maintain and strengthen the bond between mother and infant. Below: Young calves seldom stray far from their dams.

*Left: As a cow wades into deeper water to feed, her tiny calf patiently waits along the shore.
A few pleading bleats immediately bring the mother back to console her youngster.
Below: A yearling that may have patiently waited outside the periphery of the cow's birth
territory rejoins the cow and the new sibling.*

CHAPTER THREE

Water World

BY THE TIME THE SLEEPY WHISTLES of the white-throat serenade summer's return, the vibrant blooms of spring have long since faded into the darkness of the leafed-out forest. Hordes of biting flies, their wings finally freed from the confines of pupal prisons, drown out the evening choruses with their steady drone. During this season of light and warmth, moose spend a large part of their time near or in the water. Travel by canoe through moose country is bound to be enriched by close encounters with these superb animals. The electrifying thrill of silently slipping around an oxbow of a tranquil stream and suddenly encountering the looming form of a huge bull moose thrusting his mighty head up from the depths, silver droplets cascading from his sweeping antlers and plants dripping from his mouth, is a true wilderness experience and the highlight of many a canoe trip through northern waters.

This affinity for water during the fly season has led many to speculate that moose seek out an aquatic environment as an escape from the masses of biting insects. Although the water may prove a temporary refuge, this is not the main reason for the exodus of the moose. While some moose are able to extract part of their sodium requirements from roadside ditches or mineral licks, for many moose the primary source of this valued element is found in the rich supply of aquatic plants in northern ponds, streams and lake edges. Some of these water-loving plants contain as much as five hundred times the sodium concentrations of terrestrial plants. Feeding in the water also enables the moose to cool off on hot summer days. When the aquatic plants become available in June and July, often moose can be found concentrated in particularly rich feeding areas. Hailstorm Creek in Algonquin Provincial Park is one such feeding site. I have fond memories of quietly paddling a canoe through this winding, sluggish stream and observing an astounding total of twenty-two moose feeding in only two miles (three kilometres) of waterway!

Shallow waterways, rich with water lilies and other aquatic plants, are important feeding sites in summer.

While the plants consumed include yellow pond lily, pondweed and bladderwort (*Utricularia* sp.), one that moose favor is water shield. Moose may stand along the shore to feed but usually will wade right out into the water. Occasionally, one might even temporarily disappear from view as it goes underwater to pull up a plant by its rooted stem. Moose have been reported to uproot plants in water as deep as eighteen feet (five metres).

Moose gorging on aquatic growth cannot be considered elegant diners. The water boils and bubbles as they stuff their gaping mouths full of the partially submerged vegetation. When they finally raise their saturated mouths, water gushes out and plants precariously dangle out the sides. Often a feeding moose may be heard long before it is actually seen. As they feast, moose can often be closely approached by a quiet canoeist. Opportunities for photographic studies at such times are excellent.

Through most of the summer, moose can be encountered in their watery world. A calf may forage around the shallower edges while the mother wades in deeper water. At the slightest hint of danger, however, the cow will charge back to the calf's side. I still have vivid memories from many years ago of a cow and her calf at a remote northern bog. The cow was standing in water up to her belly while the tiny calf was feeding along the shore, about seventy-five feet (twenty-three metres) from its mother. I decided to give a wolf howl to see what reaction might ensue. Before I had even completed the howl, the cow explosively dashed through the water to the calf's side. Both animals stood side by side staring intently in my direction, their huge ears held upright and pointed directly at me. After a moment of unwavering concentration, they turned and fled into the safety of the nearby forest.

Many of the water plants sought by moose can be found either in the shallow waters along lake edges or in sluggish streams. Some of the best feeding sites, however, are created through the actions of another animal. Beavers (*Castor canadensis*)

Right: Beaver ponds, with their shallow waters and plentiful supply of sodium-enriched plants, offer excellent feeding opportunities.

Below: As a cow moose reaches for a mouthful of aquatic growth, biting flies cover her back and rump. While it has been speculated that these insects are the driving force behind the exodus of moose into northern waters, undoubtedly the primary impetus in many cases is the quest for water plants.

Left: Moose wade into the water to reach the succulent growth.

Right: Submerged plants may require underwater searching; frequently the head, and occasionally the entire body, is completely out of sight.

Bottom: Deeper waterways may provide not only delectable food but also temporary relief from extreme heat and biting insects.

Although plant growth is an important part of the diet by this time of the year, calves such as this set of twins still occasionally nurse until at least the end of August and occasionally into mid-September. Note the scabs on the back of the cow's legs: although the initial cause of the sores is unknown, biting flies keep the wounds open.

generate ponds by building dams. These ponds not only afford safe havens for beavers but also provide suitable sites for the water plants on which moose feed. Thus, an evening spent quietly sitting at the edge of a beaver pond may offer rewarding views of moose, as well as sightings of the large rodents that inhabit the pond. A beaver pond rich in aquatic growth may entice a number of moose; I have watched as many as nine moose feeding in a single beaver pond.

Summer is a time of plenty for most living creatures, moose not excluded. Lush green leaves, stripped from the branches of shrubs, and tender new twigs supplement their diet of aquatic plants. The fresh growth is consumed in astounding amounts — up to sixty pounds (twenty-seven kilograms) in one day! Moose grow quickly: they have been said to exhibit the most rapid growth of any large animal in America. By the end of summer, their weight will have increased substantially, in some cases reaching, and occasionally exceeding, two hundred pounds (ninety kilograms). Along with their weight, their size has also increased dramatically, and they may stand as high as three to four feet (one to one-plus metres) at the shoulder. The pale coloration of the calf, once so distinct from the dam, has now been replaced by darker browns, making them appear more like a small adult than the infant of spring, with the exception of the still relatively short face.

As summer progresses, the antlers of the bulls continue to lengthen and expand. Antler development depends, in part, on the age of the bull. Yearlings usually develop little more than slightly forked spikes, while more mature bulls develop the broad palms and long points, or tines, that give the antlers their distinctive form. An incredible investment of nutrients, such as protein, calcium and phosphorus, goes into the production of these elaborate ornaments. In fact, it has been said the amount of resources used by a bull in growing a full set of antlers can equal the amount invested by a cow in the production of an offspring. Due to the enormous

Top: Like some prehistoric creature rising from the deep, a bull thrusts its head above the surface, scattering water in all directions. Bottom: Biting flies adorn the face of an unperturbed cow as she gorges on water shield.

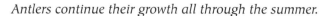

investment required, an animal weakened by disease or injury may not be able to produce the size of antlers that it could if it were healthy. And as the largest antlers are borne by animals in their prime, between six and ten years of age, the size of the rack reflects both the physical and the social status of the bull.

The plush coat of velvet covers the antlers all through the summer. While the antlers are maturing, growth is sporadic, with periods of rapid increase followed by periods of lesser development. The velvet's striking pattern of alternating light and dark bands, somewhat reminiscent of the growth rings of a tree, reflects this fragmented growth.

An injury to an antler in the velvet stage could result in a deformity. It is not rare to see a bull moose, particularly a younger animal, with one perfect antler on one side of his head and an antler bearing a much different appearance on the opposite side. However, unless the injury is to the pedicle, the structure on which the antlers begin to grow, the deformity will usually vanish when new antlers appear the following year. The rich supply of nerve endings permeating the velvet provides a sensitivity that actually acts as a deterrent against careless actions that could result in a deforming injury.

Throughout August, the lush greens of mid-summer are gradually replaced by the sombre browns of an approaching autumn. Bird song that once filled the morning and evening air is now reduced to a mere whisper. By the time the contorted pulsations of the aurora borealis begin to paint the late August nights, a strange uneasiness has begun to affect the bull moose, a restlessness that heralds the advent of the rut.

Right: Due to spurts of antler growth, the velvet cloaking the antlers acquires a banded appearance.
Below: The soft velvet continuously feeds nourishment to the growing bone beneath and is permeated with sensitive nerves.

Left: By mid-summer, the shabby appearance due to spring molt has disappeared, replaced by a dark, sleek coat of guard hairs.

Right: Terrestrial plants, much higher in nutritional value than the sodium-rich aquatic plants, become a more important food item by late summer.

Bottom: As summer passes, the large palms, the broad antler expanses, of a mature bull develop.

Left: Rich feeding sights draw numbers of moose.
Right: Although active throughout much of the night and day, early mornings and, as seen here, evenings are the best times for observing moose.

Below: By the end of summer, feeding activity lessens, and a strange restlessness overcomes the bulls.

CHAPTER FOUR

The Rut

THE CHOKING MIST SLOWLY RISES from the frost-laden vegetation into the warming glow of the awakening sun. As the first illuminating rays cut through the haze, the brackens sparkle with the light dancing across the crystals of ice deposited during the frigid night. The chilling silence, previously softly disturbed only by the distant babble of migrating geese, is now suddenly shattered by a penetrating nasal "uuuuuurrrrnnn-ungh." A crash of vegetation announces the arrival of a living form, but through the blanket of fog the ghostly spires of distant firs and spruces are all that are visible. Through the gloom the clamor draws ever nearer. At last, a towering form looms into view. It stands over seven feet (two metres) tall, and in catching the first rays of light, the massive rack of bone adorning its head glows an eerie orange. As it plods closer, the gentle nodding of the great antlers seems to keep time with its short, guttural "uuawunk" or "gawunk" calls. When the mighty bull advances, lured by the human imitation of a desiring cow, one's heart loudly pounds against the chest and blood surges through the veins. The rut has begun.

Most of the year, moose are relatively silent animals. However, during the breeding season, the rut, their silence is broken. Moose courtship is elaborate, consisting not only of intricate vocalizations but also of elegant visual displays and subtle chemical stimuli. Still, much of the underlying mechanism of the rut has yet to be resolved, for we are just beginning to unravel the complexities of this ageless ritual.

Several weeks before the actual rut commences, the bulls begin to change both in appearance and in behavior. By late August, the antlers that have been growing the previous months have reached their maximum size. The once essential velvet has served its purpose, and now in its redundancy begins to peel off. To accelerate its removal, the bulls rub and thrash their antlers against small trees and shrubs. Broken limbs and shredded bark are sure signs of the advent of this pre- or false

The rut period is characterized by frosty, mist-shrouded mornings.

Smashed limbs and shredded bark pay silent homage to
the power of a thrashing bull. Bulls may thrash initially
to assist in velvet removal, but thrashing is also
important in communication between moose.

rut. As the velvet is removed, blood emanating from the pores of the bone beneath and plant juices from the damaged vegetation combine to lend an orange-brown tint to the newly polished antlers.

Bulls in their prime usually lose their velvet first, in contrast to the less mature "teens," which keep the plush coating two to three weeks longer. Just as the size of the antlers reflects to some degree the age of the bull, the darkening of the face with the advent of the rut reflects the maturity of the animal. The face becomes black in animals six years of age or older. During the pre-rut, social ranking is established by sparring matches. These contests, consisting of antlers knocking and pushing on antlers, seldom result in injury. They eventually allow the bulls to assess visually another's rank by its antlers' dimensions, thus avoiding risky combat during later confrontations.

Generally by Labour Day weekend (the end of August) in Algonquin Provincial Park, the largest bulls have removed the last of the velvet and are responsive to the calls of a female. By simulating the long, nasal bawling song of a cow in heat, bulls within hearing distance (up to one and a half miles, or two kilometres) are easily summoned. Although birch-bark horns and even tin cans with a string pulled through produce excellent renditions, by pinching my nose and cupping my hands around my mouth, I can capture the nasal and drawn-out aspects of a cow call superbly. As the cows are not yet calling for bulls during the pre-rut, there is no competition to offset the drawing powers of a human imitation. Because bulls tend to be most active from late evening through the night and into the following morn, one of the best times to call for them is just after sunrise. In the early morn, the air is crisp and usually calm, and sound carries well. The rendition of a cow call not only travels farther but the distant approach of an excited bull is also more easily detected at this time.

Right: In the early morning mist a mighty bull prepares to thrash a shrub to announce his prowess to the world.

Below: By the end of August, the antlers have reached their maximum size. A young bull has lost most of the velvet that covers the antlers during their growth. Only a few strips lifelessly hang on.

Left: By thrashing their antlers against shrubbery, bulls announce their stature. The sound produced by antlers striking wood differs with the size of the antlers, thus perhaps enabling both cows and other bulls to determine the stature of the thrashing bull.

Below: An injury to an antler during its growth results in a deformity. The split ear on the same side of the bull's head as the damaged antler is suggestive of a rather serious injury. However, if the pedicle is not damaged, next year's antler may lack this deformity.

While bulls may be readily enticed by human imitations during the pre-rut, once the cows approach estrus and begin vocalizing during the actual rut, the same does not hold. Cows stake out small territories and call from sites known as breeding arenas. Usually these are open sites, often bog edges, old burns or beaver meadows with a surrounding ridge of forested land. From the arena, except for a midday resting period, the cow calls through the night and most of the day, patrolling the boundary of the arena and urinating excessively. Wandering bulls, which can detect these penetrating calls from great distances, hasten towards the source. The most frequent calls come from a cow in the "attractive" phase of the estrus period, a day or two before actual ovulation.

As a hopeful bull saunters into the arena, he repeatedly utters a guttural "gawunk." Saliva drools from his mouth, and he repeatedly flips his pink tongue, seemingly signalling his sexual appetite. While he appears to be drooling in anticipation of events to come, this action may actually assist in spreading into the surrounding air his salivary sex pheromones. With our blunted sense of smell, we can only guess as to the information transmitted via these pheromones. The cow also passes information of her status to bulls with the scent molecules, both by calling and by frequently urinating in her arena. A bull keys in on the odors, sniffing the air and the ground, even taking some of the pheromone-containing urine into his mouth. To analyze better the composition of these airborne odors, the bull raises his head with gaping mouth, flared nostrils and curled upper lip. This posture, known as flemen, enables increased olfactory perception by exposing the chemical signals to the vomeronasal organ in the palate of his mouth. This organ in turn transmits signals via nerves to those centers in the brain responsible for sexual behavior. A bull investigating the cow's chemical communique is somewhat reminiscent of a wine taster swirling a sample around in his or her mouth to evaluate its subtle characteristics more effectively (although the wine taster lacks the advantage of that specialized organ).

Once a bull begins attending a cow, the visual and olfactory stimuli the cow presents tend to keep the bull close at hand. A human imitation of a cow, however realistic, fails to draw him away from his mate's side.

However relatively simple this mating system may appear, it is anything but. When bulls are enticed by the calls of a cow, they may announce their arrival by thrashing their antlers against shrubs and small trees. Different sizes of antlers produce different qualities of sound as they strike wood. This sound may not only serve to notify other bulls of the size and vigor of the animal thrashing but may also serve to impress the cow. As the courting bull approaches the cow, his antlers are prominently displayed, permitting her to assess his rank and fitness. Bulls also communicate their status through chemical signals, and the antlers may be employed in the dispensing of these odors. Using its front feet, a bull digs out a shallow depression, a "rut pit," into the ground. Into this rut or wallow pit he urinates, and into the odiferous mixture of urine and sex pheromones he rolls, covering himself in his own perfume. Cows in heat may also roll in the bull's pit, thereby picking up his pheromones, which help to accelerate the ovulation process.

If two bulls are enticed to a cow's arena, a fascinating interaction results. Spectacular stories of bulls battling to the death, uprooting towering trees in their struggle, permeate popular magazines. While these astounding tales appeal to our propensity for sensationalism, in reality the contests are highly ritualized and considerably less violent. When two bulls are vying for the favors of the same cow, they confront each other initially not with aggression but with dramatic, elegant displays. To enable visual assessment of their respective ranks, they slowly swing their great antlers from side to side or bow their heads to the ground. In the case of

Left: Cows mark their arenas with chemical advertisements in the form of pheromones in their urine. Readily airborne, these pheromones not only help to attract bulls but also to pass on information as to a cow's sexual state.

Below: Fragments of shrubbery, dislodged during a thrashing episode, cling to the antlers of a young bull. These ornaments tend to be quickly discarded with the next episode of thrashing.

unequal rank, only a young, inexperienced bull would dare to risk confrontation. Normally, however, the lesser bull will retreat or will try to appease its superior with an appropriate gesture by turning away.

During the rut, a bull regards the surrounding area as its "personal zone," the size of this zone reflecting the rank of the bull. An encroachment upon this personal zone can be considered an act of aggression. To prevent "trespassing" into this zone, a bull signals his position by loudly thrashing shrubbery with the antlers or by uttering a tremendous bellowing roar, reportedly similar to the scream of a charging tiger. Because larger bulls may thrash more intensely than lesser bulls and because large antlers, when striking wood, produce a sound distinctly different than that produced by smaller antlers, thrashing may serve to communicate additional information as to the bull's status.

If the challenger is not intimidated by these displays, with a swaying, stiff gait it will cross the boundary of its opponent's personal zone. Both bulls then face each other, slowly swinging their great antlers from side to side. At first they carefully eye each other's adornments, then cautiously make contact with them. Finally, with heads down and antlers raised, they powerfully shove against each other, trying to push the opponent back in defeat. Battles are often short-lived, but if the bulls are relatively equal in strength, a confrontation may last up to half an hour, or even longer. After a lengthy battle, exhausted, the combatants must rest to regain their strength. While reports of such battles have been frequently glamorized by details of mortal wounds, the injuries sustained are rarely serious. Although the lower branches, or the brow tines, of the antlers of prime bulls protect the eyes during such confrontations, an inadequate shield by the brow tines may lead to injuries of the skin or, even more seriously, blindness. Rarely will antlers fatally lock, and probably of equal rarity will a puncture to a vital part of the body be inflicted.

Wallow or rut pits, dug by bulls, are first urinated in, then wallowed in. By rolling around in his pit, the bull spreads urine containing pheromones over his head and body, providing himself with a unique olfactory badge. Cows may also roll in a bull's pit to scent themselves with his pheromones.

Right: With head thrust forward, an amorous and hopeful bull approaches a young cow. The velvet dangling from the antler indicates that this scenario is taking place in the pre-rut, a time when cows are not yet receptive.

Bottom: Completely unreceptive, she rejects his advances, with ears laid back to indicate her displeasure. During his approach, the cow keeps her backside away from the desiring bull. Not until the actual rut will this bull find a receptive cow.

*Left: When two prime bulls encounter each other, rank is
advertised through head gestures. If one bull is subordinate, it
will present its head sideways or retreat, thereby defusing
aggression on the part of the dominant bull.*

When a cow begins calling prior to her estrus, she is in the "attractive" phase. Bulls, drawn in by her persistent calls, try to woo her with their antlers and sex pheromones. If the proper stimuli are present, the cow will allow the bull close approach. She then signals her entry into the "proceptive" phase by permitting the bull to sniff and lick her genital area. This act stimulates her further towards ovulation and the "receptive" phase. It also allows the bull to determine the approach of that phase in which copulation is permitted. However, before the arrival of the proceptive phase, the bull is not permitted intimate contact. I have watched a cow, unappreciative of a bull's advances, continually turn her back-end away from the bull, facing him with ears laid back to display her displeasure. At one point she even leapt backwards in an effort to escape his lustful intentions.

During the proceptive phase, the bull stays close to the cow. Throughout foreplay leading up to the main event, caresses are frequently exchanged between the pair. The bell of the bull may play a role in the transmission of sex pheromones, for the cow will thrust her neck and head under the head of the bull. As the time for breeding approaches, the bull rests his head on her back and rump. This placement of the bull's head, known as chinning, may serve to transfer his pheromones to the cow, as well as to test the cow for weight receptiveness. Mounting is quickly performed, with copulation lasting only a few seconds. Actual mating is rarely witnessed, particularly in the heavily forested regions where the woodland moose roams. I have been extremely fortunate to have witnessed it on one occasion. The thrusts of the bull were so strong that the cow lurched forward, causing the bull to jump froglike on his back legs while trying to maintain his position. This brief act, only seconds in duration, was repeated three times over a period of approximately forty minutes.

Bulls closely attend their cows throughout the two- to three-day period leading up to and including their receptive phase. During this time, the calf — if the cow

has one — will remain in the vicinity of the pair. When a bull, cow and calf are seen together during the rut, the association is frequently misinterpreted as a close-knit family group. However, this congregation is very short-lived for, once the cow is no longer receptive to the bull and she repudiates him continually, he eventually wanders off in search of other receptive females. There is even a strong possibility that another bull the previous year sired the offspring. These bull-cow associations disappear after the rut, and the cows, with calves in tow, face the rest of the year unattended.

Bulls in rut have often been reported to be highly unpredictable and dangerous. While there have been confirmed cases of bulls chasing and killing humans and attacking vehicles during the breeding season, this is not common and fatalities are very rare. Over the years, I have spent considerable time in moose country during the mating season. Not only have I lured in bulls with female imitations, but I also have promoted aggressiveness by thrashing antlers and uttering bull calls. Despite having called in literally hundreds of bulls, only once have I been charged. This one experience, though, was certainly more than enough to drive a permanent wedge of respect into me, a respect that rises to the surface whenever a magnificent bull begins to approach.

It was a cold, blustery morning in early October. Graham Forbes, a friend conducting wolf research in the area, accompanied me on a "moosing" expedition. Shortly after sunrise, we encountered a prime bull with a cow. We spent nearly an hour studying and photographing the pair without incident. At one point I was about fifty feet (fifteen metres) from the bull, and his hulking frame nearly filled the scene in the viewfinder of the camera. Suddenly, he lowered his massive antlers and charged. My heart leapt into my throat, and I grabbed the tripod with mounted camera, fleeing in terror. As the pounding of his great hooves drew nearer and

As a bull approaches a cow, his tongue conspicuously lashes out. This may serve to spread his own pheromones into the air, as well as to pick up those from the cow.

nearer, panic surged through my body, for I was certain death was inevitable. Fortunately, as sudden as his charge had begun, it ended, and he returned to the cow. Eventually, I too stopped and for support held on to, appropriately, a trembling aspen as I uncontrollably shook. My heart violently pounded, seemingly almost through the wall of my chest. After several minutes, I had regained most of my composure; I cautiously approached again — foolishly perhaps. As I encroached once more upon his personal zone, he charged. Again, I hastily and fearfully retreated; but, as in the first instance, the charge ended shortly after I had fled.

Why the aggressive behavior and why the sudden termination of his charges? Soon after, it became clear this bull was actually breeding with the cow. As far as I was able to interpret, he was chasing away any possible threat that infringed upon his personal zone while he attended to his mate. However, he did not wish to leave her unattended for any length of time, for her period of receptiveness had arrived; he could not risk her exploitation by another bull in his absence. My hasty retreat satisfied his desire to drive off any threat, hence his short-lived pursuit. Once breeding had occurred, the cow lay down to rest and the bull stood sentinel over her. After unintentionally eliciting a third charge, one in which the bull forced me to dive into a thick tangle of balsam fir, resulting in bloodied face and arms and a broken tripod, we decided we had foolishly pushed the bull to the limits of his tolerance. Quickly but quietly, we moved back through the forest, leaving the pair in privacy.

While at times moose may appear to be complacent, accommodating animals, we must respect their physical superiority. One glancing blow from those massive feet would be all that is necessary to crush the life from our fragile bodies. How a moose interprets our outlines and movements is unknown; therefore, it is always wise to keep a safe distance when admiring one of these giants of the north, no matter how docile and harmless it may appear.

The rut is, to my mind, the most exciting and fascinating aspect of moose biology. This is the season when elaborate, complex and elegant behaviors emerge, behaviors concealed the rest of the year. The rut is an annual ritual, precipitated by the photoperiod, or the amount of daylight. In a population where prime bulls are numerous, most of the cows get bred during their first estrus. If, however, there is a shortage of bulls, not all cows may breed during their first heat. Unbred cows are capable of entering estrus up to at least four times, each spaced by at least three weeks, but each estrus is often progressively weaker and the length of time separating them fluctuates. Cows entering a late estrus are more likely to entice a younger, inferior bull as a mate, as prime bulls are usually unresponsive towards the end of the rut.

As the rut progresses, the brilliant hues of autumn gradually evanesce. Late morning winds color the air with bastions of painted leaves, snatching and tossing them from their lofty perches, eventually discarding them into the death grip of the earth beneath. As sex hormone levels drop and the final driving impulses of the rut relinquish their hold, the bulls return to a state of celibacy. Instinctively, they begin to prepare for the hardships of the fast-approaching season, a season when all life is tested but only the fittest survive.

In a posture known as flemen, a bull tests for airborne chemical signals from the cow. This posture exposes the sensitive vomeronasal organ in the roof of the mouth to any pheromones that may be present.

A cow selects the bull with which she breeds. Antler size and shape and pheromones are all important cues that advertise the bull's suitability as a potential mate.

A bull closely watches over a cow approaching estrus.
Several days may be spent together before breeding occurs,
with the bull ensuring that other bulls do not interfere with
his opportunity to do so.

Below: When in her proceptive phase, the cow allows the bull to smell and lick her genital region. This enables the bull to determine how near to ovulation she is, and also stimulates the cow into her receptive phase, in which ovulation and copulation occur.

Right: Under the protective blanket of darkness, copulation is swiftly performed. Lasting only seconds, the slow speed of the camera shutter captures only a blurred record.

Left: Although most contests between bulls do not end in serious injury, fatalities occasionally occur. This bull, with a puncture through its side into the gut, may have been a rare victim of the rut.
Below: During the rut, calves stay in the vicinity of their dams. Although this appears to be a family group, it is not, and the bull's association ends shortly after the cow leaves estrus. The odds are low that he is the actual father of her present offspring.

Right: Dr. Anthony Bubenik, seen here calling with a birch-bark horn, studied the social significance of moose antlers by wearing a dummy bull moose head during the rut. His innovative studies have provided us with most of our knowledge of antler significance and their communicative powers. To his right, Peter Smith of the Ontario Ministry of Natural Resources thrashes a small tree, hoping to elicit a response from a bull.

Below: If a cow is not bred on her first estrus, she enters a second, and even a third or fourth if she still is not successful in attracting a mate.

Left: With the passing of the rut by mid- to late October, moose concentrate on feeding and building up their energy reserves before winter's harsh arrival.

Right: Young bulls, such as this yearling, are sexually active but usually do not get the opportunity to breed since older and more physically superior bulls and discriminating cows deny them such an opportunity.

Below: The rut is an extremely complex and fascinating phenomenon.

Below and right: By the time that the maples have dropped their leaves, and birches and poplars have turned to gold, the peak of the rut has passed.

CHAPTER FIVE

Season of Endurance

HARDWOOD HILLS, ONCE ABLAZE with the flames of autumnal splendor, now stand stark and sombre against the cold blue sky. The incessant chatter of roving finches echoes from the sheltering stands of conifers. By the time winter snows begin to smother the frozen landscape, many creatures have already disappeared into their subterranean burrows to slumber away the frigid months to come. But for others, including the moose, winter presents a physical challenge, an ultimate test of endurance and survival and one that may prove fatal for the ill-prepared.

As the blinding ascendancy of the rut begins to fade, moose focus their attention upon replenishing fat reserves before the onslaught of winter's fury. Having lost up to thirty percent of their body weight during their lustful and relatively food-free wanderings, the bulls now concentrate on feasting and resting, restoring their depleted energy reserves.

By mid-December, many of the prime bulls have already dropped their head ornamentation. Antlers, once a symbol of vigor and strength, have lost their significance and now serve only as an unnecessary burden to bear. During the rut, high levels of the male hormone testosterone result in the maintenance of the connection between the dead bone of the antlers and the living bone of the pedicle. When the rut is finished, the testosterone level drops, providing the impetus for the casting of the antlers. As the connection between living and dead bone begins to abate and as the skin underneath the coronets of the dead antlers begins to swell, bulls start to rub their antlers against the bark of trees as if to relieve some unpleasant itchiness in the pedicles. Freshly debarked trees signal the prelude to antler casting. Bulls in their prime tend to be the first to breed, the first to come out of rut and, consequently, the first to drop their antlers. Younger individuals, who entered the rut too late to be successful suitors, still maintain high levels of testosterone and

The luxuriant winter coat of a moose is essential for protection against winter's chill. Initially quite dark, the coat is bleached to this soft brown by late winter.

hence retain their antlers into January or February, while yearlings may keep theirs into March.

If a bull holds a high rank and is in a state of well-being, both antlers are usually shed synchronously. They may fall anywhere from at approximately the same time to a few hours apart, and thus may be found directly opposite on either side of the bull's tracks in the snow or up to several hundred feet (a hundred metres) apart. In other cases, it may be days or weeks before both are cast, and a bull may attempt to accelerate the removal of a stubborn antler by knocking it against vegetation. Antlers lying on the ground soon lose their perfect form for they are frequently gnawed upon for their calcium content by many types of rodents, including mice, squirrels and porcupines. Deer and moose have also been known to nibble cast antlers for their valuable mineral content.

At first, it may seem an incredible waste of resources for a bull moose to discard his antlers annually, only to grow them anew the following year. However, by growing a new set each year, the bull is permitted to advertize his continuing maturation and elevation in social ranking, which usually correlates with age and his status of the previous year. If an antler grew deformed from an injury during its development, the malformation may disappear with subsequent antler replacement, although a more serious injury may require from three to five subsequent antler cycles before the deformity disappears completely. As the antlers can be a considerable weight to carry around — up to sixty pounds (twenty-seven kilograms) or more for a large set — the loss of these just prior to the physical stresses of winter undoubtedly offers some survival advantage to the bull.

Winter can be a time of great physical duress, with temperatures occasionally plunging below minus forty degrees. Just as we humans pull on an extra layer of undergarments to combat the cold, the moose also adds an additional layer of insula-

Young bulls, still maintaining high levels of testosterone, spar into the early winter. Older and more mature bulls usually have cast their antlers and any sexual behavior by this time.

Young maples are often browsed while snow depth still allows easy access to these food resources.

Winter droppings are pellet-shaped due to the relatively dry content of the needles and twigs of trees and shrubs.

tion for warmth. During the fall, an undercoat of fine, kinky hairs begins to grow beneath the longer, coarser guard hairs. Also, the outer coat is reinforced with longer, brownish guard hairs, providing a thick, luxuriant appearance; these hairs bleach into light brown as winter progresses. This barrier of hair renders protection against the savage elements the moose must face during the most trying season of all.

As winter snows continue to accumulate, the long legs of the moose allow it to cross most terrain easily. Frozen waterways now provide shorter and novel routes to new feeding areas. While these alternate routes offer unobstructed mobility, an underlying hazard is involved. Moose that venture onto these highways of ice too early or too late in the season risk breaking through and becoming trapped. But once the ice provides a solid footing, lake edges and rivers are frequently exploited as travel corridors.

Throughout the summer months, moose tend to utilize a fairly small area, often less than four square miles (ten square kilometres), but during the winter the size of the home range is even more reduced. Often, several small, heavily used areas may be selected. The favored feeding sites of earlier seasons are now abandoned, for the plants found in those sites are no longer available.

Long gone is the lush growth of summer. Moose now depend on the twigs of trees and shrubs and the needles of conifers for nourishment. In many regions, particularly in northwestern North America, willows and red osier dogwood are the primary food. In others, trembling aspen or white birch is preferred. In some areas, such as northern Ontario, the twigs and needles of balsam fir are the mainstay during the cold winter months. The extremity of the twig, bearing the past seasons' growth, offers the greatest nutritional reward for moose. However, in heavily browsed or low-quality feeding areas, moose may be forced to browse farther back on the twigs, feeding on growth two or three years old, which is low in nutritional value.

Below: These magnificent antlers are usually cast shortly after the first snows of winter begin to accumulate. Note that the skin at the base of the antler has been rubbed, indicating antler casting is near.

Right: Before their antlers are cast, bulls rub them against trees. This action apparently relieves an itchiness that develops at the antler base prior to the loss of the antlers.
Far Right: Antlers may be dropped almost synchronously or several days apart, depending on the stature of the bull.

With temperatures plummeting well below freezing, with biting winds adding a razor's edge to the cold and with deepening snow draining energy at every step taken, winter tests the fortitude of any living creature. However, for much of the adversity that this season presents, moose have little problem coping. Only when the wind chill drops the temperature below minus twenty degrees Fahrenheit (minus thirty degrees Celsius) or when the snow depth exceeds three to four feet (one metre) does the moose begin to feel the effects of this cruel season. With its towering reach, moose are able to browse the vegetation up to twelve feet (three and a half metres) from the ground. As the snows deepen, access to slightly higher browse may be achieved, but on those rare occasions when a hard crust enables the moose to wander on top of this white blanket, entire new horizons of food, untouched during previous winters, become accessible.

However, if normal conditions prevail and if moose have wintered in an area for numerous years, high-quality browse may be scarce. Moose must then sustain themselves on inferior foods. Under these conditions and if excessive energy is being spent to attain food, the relative fitness of the animals will be lowered. Bulls and barren cows first use fat and, later, muscle reserves to survive this ecological trial. Pregnant cows, protecting the unborn resources they must nourish during this season, are apparently able to maximize their digestive capabilities, thus gleaning more energy from low-quality foods and therefore surviving without totally depleting their fat reserves. But under severe conditions of starvation, the physiological stress may be extreme, affecting not only the calving success of the pending spring but also perhaps reducing the cow's reproductive capacity the following year.

For much of the year, moose live either as relatively solitary animals or with a temporary companion of the same sex. Calves remain with their dams throughout their first winter, and occasionally last year's offspring, now yearlings, also follow

A young bull, probably only a year and a half old, beds down on a hardwood slope.

along. Thus, small family groups develop. However, small concentrations of non-related moose can also be encountered in good feeding areas. While the white-tailed deer forms winter groupings in sheltered areas known as "yards" as a response to decreased mobility, moose concentrations are usually due to the local availability of food. For the most part, these groupings should not be identified as "yards." Because of their incredibly long legs, moose are usually not restricted in their movements to snow less than forty inches (one hundred centimetres) deep. However, deep snows bearing a thin, hard crust can restrict mobility, forcing moose to seek the shelter of coniferous cover, such as hemlock (*Tsuga canadensis*), and thus possibly becoming concentrated in sites that could be deemed temporary "yards."

Through the seemingly endless northern winter, moose do little more than eat and rest. In feeding areas, trails form mazes through the snow, and rounded depressions indicate bedding sites. For much of the winter, darkness dominates the light. But gradually the days lengthen, and with the inevitable approach of the vernal equinox, the sun begins to burn with ever-increasing intensity. Snow levels grudgingly recede, and awakening buds begin to swell. Within the veins of trees, sap begins to flow more freely, transporting nutrients to the growing tissues. By late winter, if the browse supply has dwindled, moose begin to nibble or strip the bark off certain trees, in particular from red maples, striped maples and trembling aspen. The distinctive marks left on the trees is often attributed by the uninitiated to bears marking their territories with their claws! Breaking into the bark with their bottom front teeth, a moose will grasp the loose end and, with an upward swing of the head, rip it free. The use of bark is actually a common feeding strategy in most of the deer species, for the nutritive value of this woody material equals that of hay of mediocre quality. In addition, bark is also a source of unfrozen water, an item of great energetic value during the frigid months.

Below: Occasionally, travel along waterways may prove to be a fatal error if the ice cannot bear the weight. However, nothing is ever wasted, as scavenging wolves and ravens exploit the riches of the carcass.

Right: The long legs of moose permit travel through most snow-covered terrain.

Winter taxes the fortitude of any living creature that dares to challenge its power. It is an unforgiving season, and an animal that exhibits any weakness will be severely reprimanded. While some mortality occurs every winter, often the unfortunate are those moose weakened by accidents, disease or parasites. The survivors reap the bounties of spring, and the arrival of a new generation promises a continuance of the monarch of the north.

Moose roam freely through hardwood forests in early winter, but tend to frequent coniferous areas during the main part of this trying season.

Right: Moose may use hemlocks or other conifers for cover during harsher conditions. These evergreen trees tend to act as umbrellas, reducing the amount of snow below them. They also provide a warmer site in which to shelter.

Below: In late winter, a moose strips off the bark of a red maple when other foods become increasingly harder to find. Bark does contain some nutritional value and also offers a source of water.

CHAPTER SIX

Relationships

MOOSE IN ITS PRIME has little to fear from most predators, for few animals apart from man possess the ability to kill it. Timber wolves (*Canis lupus*) tend to take either calves separated from their mothers or sick or disabled animals. There are recorded accounts of adult moose standing their ground and successfully fending off entire packs of wolves. The front feet of a moose, as well as its hind ones, are lethal weapons that will take their toll on unwary adversaries. Wolves, opportunists by nature, often scavenge on moose that have died from other causes. In so doing, they often are erroneously blamed for causing the demise of those moose.

Black bears (*Ursus americanus*), being rather small bears, tend to prey primarily on newborns or exceptionally young moose. In western North America, Grizzly bears (*Ursus arctos*), larger and more powerful than their dark relatives, have been known on occasion to take adult moose, particularly in late winter when they leave their dens and the crusty snow hinders a moose's movements. As a rule, however, these large predators seem to have little negative effect on moose populations and in some ways may be deemed beneficial by removing animals in poor or diseased condition.

Perhaps the most serious, rather sinister threat to moose comes not from large predators, such as bears and wolves, but from a rather surprising source — the white-tailed deer (*Odocoileus virginianus*). Where the ranges of moose and white-tailed deer overlap in North America, moose frequently develop a fatal illness commonly known as moose disease. Moose infected with this disease may appear unusually tame, walk in circles, bump into objects because of impaired eyesight and coordination and drag their back legs because of paralysis.

Although it might be surprising that the parasitic roundworm responsible for these effects is transferred from deer to moose, it seems inconceivable that a third animal, a "lowly" slug or snail, is responsible for this transfer! The adult parasite

Due to its immense stature and strength, a mature moose has few natural predators.

survives quite nicely in the spaces and sinuses of the head of the white-tailed deer, with negligible effect on its host. Eggs are carried by the blood into the lungs, where they develop into larvae. From here the larvae subsequently pass up the trachea, only to be swallowed and eventually pass through the deer, ending up with the droppings. When a slug or snail stops to savor the moist droppings, the larva penetrates this intermediate host through its foot. The slug, carrying the parasite inside, returns to feed on foliage. A browsing moose gets more than it bargains if it inadvertently swallows the infected slug along with the foliage. The parasite leaves the slug and penetrates the moose's stomach, eventually entering the spinal tract. Here it begins to damage the nervous system as it works towards the brain. Incredibly, it takes only one tiny roundworm to immobilize and kill a one thousand pound (four hundred and fifty kilograms) moose. For such a tiny animal, the parasite has a rather complicated name — *Parelaphostrongylus tenuis*. Fortunately, its common name, brain or meningeal worm, is considerably easier to articulate.

The brain worm story is an excellent example of how different animals indirectly have an impact on each other. But there is another aspect to this story, one that is directly tied with man. Originally in North America the moose of the northern forest had little contact with the white-tailed deer of the southern regions. However, when white man began to clear the forests in the northeastern part of the continent, initially to establish farms and later to exploit the timber, and when raging fires cleared forest tracts, new deer habitat was created. Deer began to expand their range northward, eventually infringing upon that of the moose. When contact between these originally ecologically separated species was made, the parasite was passed to the susceptible moose.

But why does the parasite only kill moose and not the white-tailed deer? The reason lies in the history of these two animals in North America, where the white-

Although they have been credited with forcing moose out of the woods and into the water, biting flies may not be the main reason for moose to go to water. A swarm circles the head and antlers of a bull, batted occasionally by the flick of an ear.

Left: Black bears are known to kill young moose calves and may well be a primary reason that cows often give birth on islands.

Below: Few who gaze into the innocent stare of a white-tailed deer could imagine that behind those gentle eyes lies, quite literally, the greatest threat to a moose. The brain worm, a tiny nematode, is transmitted to moose indirectly from deer.

tailed deer and the brain worm appear to have evolved together. Over the eons of time of their co-existence, a relatively stable relationship formed between the two. On the other hand, moose are relative newcomers to North America, arriving only during the last ice age. As they had evolved in the Old World, where the white-tailed deer and the brain worm were not found, moose had no opportunity to develop the same resistance to the parasite that the white-tailed deer seems to enjoy. It seems ironic that moose, with all their enormity and power, should fall victim to such rather minuscule adversaries.

The brain worm creates fatal havoc with the internal mechanisms of its mighty host. But another tiny creature also causes difficulties for the moose, a parasite that, unlike the brain worm, lives on the outer surface of the moose's body.

During the autumn, as moose walk through shrubby vegetation, they unknowingly encounter tiny legs waving to and fro from the foliage. When the moose brushes against this vegetation, these active legs grab onto the passing hair and hoist a minute body onto its new haven. The traveller crawls down the ladder of hair to the base, then buries its mouthparts into the warm flesh, feasting on the life-giving blood of the moose. This parasite, a tick, is appropriately called the winter tick (*Dermacentor albipictus*) for it is found on moose only from late fall through winter until early spring. Although most years its numbers are relatively low, some years it can be a serious pest. In times of large populations, a single moose can bear tens of thousands of ticks.

Ticks seem to prefer the ears, belly, anal region and under the legs, although they can also be found on most other parts. By their feeding actions, ticks physically aggravate the moose. In an effort to relieve itself of the unwanted parasites, a moose will rub against shrubs and the rough bark of trees. Although providing some temporary relief, this action may have serious ramifications. As the animal

With their tiny heads buried deep into the raw flesh of a moose, winter ticks feast on its blood. Female ticks, soon to drop to the ground to lay their eggs, engorge to the size of a thumbnail.

vigorously rubs, the thick winter hair — of paramount importance in providing insulation against the biting cold of winter — is dislodged. Skin, often raw from the scratching efforts, is directly exposed to the elements, and heat loss is inevitable. In severe bouts of cold, particularly if accompanied by wetness, moose can, and do, perish from hypothermia. While it is possible some moose may succumb to the effects of other diseases while physically weakened by a heavy parasite load, hair loss is the main problem generated by the ticks.

In early spring the ticks drop off the host, and the females lay their myriads of eggs (several thousand or more) in masses under ground litter. The larval ticks, inactive all summer, climb the nearby vegetation in the fall, to complete their cycle on the moose. As in the case of the brain worm, the moose appears to have made contact with the winter tick only after it arrived in North America, hence the moose's lack of resistance to this external parasite, a resistance other members of the deer family seem to possess.

The effect of biting flies, such as mosquitoes (Culicidae), black flies (Simulidae) and deer and horse flies (Tabanidae), on moose is debatable. The females of these flies use the blood of the moose to nourish their developing eggs. There is circumstantial evidence that moose are driven out of the woods by these flies, seeking solace in wet places. However, the association of moose and water during fly season may be more of a coincidence than the result of a direct relationship, since moose seek aquatic plants at this time of year to rebuild their sodium reserves. If flies were the main reason for moose being in the water, one would expect fewer moose to be in the water on windy or cold days than on hot, calm days. Yet, this correlation does not always hold; in fact, at times the opposite seems to exist. However, a moose gorging on water plants generally has hordes of flies surrounding its head and rump, and the flicking of the large ears certainly seems to indicate

By rubbing against rough bark in an attempt to relieve the itching, a moose
scrapes away its insulating winter coat. If the weather turns cold and wet,
this moose could possibly die from hypothermia.

Left: Posted warnings on northern highways notify drivers of moose-crossing areas.

Right: Moose along the highway in Algonquin Park always draw big crowds. These concentrations of people and their cars are known as "moose jams."

annoyance. Whether moose enter waterways in summer in search of food, to escape flies or to cool down, lake edges, marshes and beaver ponds are superb sites for viewing these animals in that season.

While many of the flies that attack moose also seek out other animals as hosts, one small fly is quite specific to the moose. Known as the moose fly (*Haematobosca alcis*), this insect, which resembles a small house fly, feeds on the blood of moose. The adults never seem to wander far from the moose, and swarms can be found around the calcaneum, anus and hindquarters, areas with the least amount of hair. Despite their affinity for moose and despite speculation that they cause moose great stress, researchers report that the moose pay little heed to them. When a moose enters the water to feed, the flies congregate on the head and antlers. These flies are so rarely found away from moose that they probably even mate on them. Carrying their close association with moose a step further, the flies even lay their eggs in moose droppings, essential food for the larvae. Moose flies overwinter in the pupal stage, presumably in the soil, and emerge as adults in late spring.

Although moose — as with all wild animals — host a wide variety of parasites, one other parasite deserves special mention. The small tapeworm, *Echinococcus granulosus*, frequently spends its larval stage, a hydatid cyst, in the lungs, and occasionally the liver, of moose. To complete its life cycle, the parasite needs another host, a large canid, such as the timber wolf. By eating the infected organs of a moose, a wolf ingests the parasite. Once inside its final host, the adult tapeworm survives in the intestine. Its eggs pass out with the wolf's droppings and are somehow picked up by moose. As the cysts are usually more prevalent in older moose and as wolves tend to kill more frequently and eat ill or older animals or scavenge dead moose, it would appear that the parasite enhances its chances of being passed on to its final host.

Although few natural predators are capable of killing an adult moose, this generality does not include man. While in northern regions native people still use moose for food and hides, throughout much of its range the moose is hunted primarily as a source of "recreation." When one thinks of man-moose interactions, usually the aspect of the harvest by hunters comes to mind. However, another sort of interaction can occur any time of the year, and in this type of encounter the moose is not always the only loser. With their tendency to be highly active after sunset and with their dark coloration blending easily into the night, moose are difficult to discern as they cross highways. Every year numerous collisions with moose occur, often with both parties suffering devastating consequences. The best strategy when travelling at night through moose country is to drive slowly, paying particular heed to posted warnings that indicate areas of habitual moose activity. By remembering we are the intruders, we can endeavor to ensure that natural inhabitants remain unscathed by our transitory passings.

While many of the afflictions affecting moose do not cause permanent disability, as noted, some can prove fatal. Unfortunately, many people consider the death of a large animal to be tragic and believe the loss of life a waste. In the natural world, however, there is no waste. When a moose dies, every body component, whether flesh, hair or bone, is used by other living organisms. The list of animals that scavenge a moose carcass is almost endless and includes eagles, ravens, foxes, martens, fishers, wolverines and bears. The death of one moose may mean life for countless other organisms, particularly during the critical season of winter. When predators, disease, parasites or environmental stress strike, the less fit (the weakest) are usually the first to succumb. This "weeding out" of the less fit through the actions of a powerful force known as natural selection tends to result in a healthier, more fit population, which through future generations may exhibit greater resistance to those same environmental stresses.

With its long legs, dark coloration and nocturnal habits, moose pose a danger to unwary motorists.

CHAPTER SEVEN

Reflections

FOR MANY, THE MOURNFUL WAIL OF A LOON serenading a fiery sunset epitomizes the wild spirit of northern regions. For others, the haunting howl of a lone timber wolf echoing over mist-shrouded hills exemplifies this ambience of untamed country. However, the towering form of a bull moose in its prime, its great antlers glowing in the warmth of the breaking dawn, inspires in us deep emotions not only of primeval wonder but also of profound respect. As we watch in awe this giant reaching high into the overhanging limbs, our spirits soar back in time, uniting with those of past Algonkians when, in reverence, they too watched this gentle beast feeding.

The Algonkians and other native peoples formerly depended on, and in some regions still rely on, the moose for sustenance and materials. Over the millennia, they harvested this giant of the north with their primitive weaponry. When local animal numbers became depleted, they moved to new hunting grounds, thereby allowing for recuperation of overharvested populations. Thus, these early hunters lived as an integral part of the ecosystem, surviving in harmony with the other components of the northern woods.

Unfortunately, the delicate balance between man and his environment has been upset. Even though moose inhabit the northern habitats of our world, they are no longer far removed from the effects of our civilization. Throughout the entire range of the moose, we are steadily encroaching on its untamed country and degrading its natural surroundings.

It is our inherent responsibility, our moral obligation, to follow the example of the early Algonkians, ensuring not only that moose will eternally roam throughout their northern haunts but also that the wild country essential to the survival of these great beasts and the myriads of other living creatures be preserved for all generations to come.

May the autumn woods forever be alive with the lamenting cries and elegant rituals of this magnificent animal, twig eater of the north.

A symbol of the vastness and wildness of the north country, the moose is commonly referred to as "the mighty monarch of the north."

Selected References

THE LITERATURE on moose is vast. Rather than attempt to provide a comprehensive listing of all the books and articles that are available, only a few select references for specific aspects of moose biology are given.

GENERAL

Bedard, J., et al. *Alces: Moose Ecology*. Laval, Quebec: Les Presses de l'université, 1974.

Bubenik, A.B.; Timmerman, R.H.; and Saunders, B. "Simulation of Population Structure and Size in Moose on Behalf of Age and Structure of Harvested Animals." *Alces 11*, 391-463, 1975.

Bubenik, A.B. "Behaviour of Moose (*Alces alces* spp.) of North America." *Swedish Wildlife Research Suppl.* 1: 333-365, 1987.

Peterson, R.L. *North American Moose*. Toronto: University of Toronto Press, 1955.

ANTLERS

Bubenik, A.B. "The Behavioral Aspects of Antlerogenesis." In: Brown, R.D. (ed). *Antler Development in Cervidae*. C. Kleberg Wildlife Research Institute, 1982.

Putnam, R. *The Natural History of Deer*. Christopher Helm Publishers Ltd, 1988. (See pages 134-152.)

MINERAL LICKS

Jones, R.L.; and Hanson, H.C., *Mineral Licks, Geography and Biogeochemistry of North American Ungulates*. The Iowa State University Press, 1988.

Parasites and Diseases

Anderson, R.C.; and Lankester M.W. "Infectious and Parasitic Diseases and Arthropod Pests of Moose in North America." *Naturaliste can.,* 101: 23-50, 1974.

Burger, J.F.; and Anderson J.R. "Taxonomy and Life History of the Moose Fly, *Haematobosca alcis,* and its Association with the Moose, *Alces alces shirasi* in Yellowstone National Park." *Ann. Ent. Soc. Amer.* 67: 204-214, 1974.

Lankester, M.W.; and Sein, R.D. "The Moose Fly, *Haematobosca alcis,* (Muscidae) and Skin Lesions on *Alces alces.*" Alces *22*: 361-375, 1986.

Predators

Mech, L.D. *The Wolf: The Ecology and Behaviour of an Endangered Species.* American Museum of Natural History and Natural History Press, 1970.

Messier, F.; and Crete M. "Moose-Wolf Dynamics and the Natural Regulation of Moose Populations." *Oecologia 65*: 503-512, 1985.

Peterson, R.O. *Ecological Studies of Wolves on Isle Royale. Annual Report - 1986, 1987.* Department of Biological Science, Michigan Technological University. Houghton, 1987.

The Rut

Bubenik, A.B. "Behavioral Significance of the Moose Bell." *Alces 119*: 238-245, 1984.

Bubenik, A.B. "Behavior of Moose (*Alces alces* spp.) of North America." *Swedish Wildlife Research Suppl. 1*: 333-365, 1987.

Lent, P.C. "A Review of Rutting Behavior in Moose." *Naturaliste can., 101*: 307-323, 1974.

Glossary

Antlers deciduous bony structures that grow annually on the heads of bull moose. They are used as visual symbols of their social ranking and status and play an important role in the breeding season.

Arena an open area, often an old bog, beaver meadow or forest clearing, which a cow moose uses for its breeding territory during the rut.

Attractive Phase the early phase in the estrus cycle of the cow moose, in which she calls and urinates excessively in an arena to attract a potential mate.

Bell the skin flap that dangles from the throat of a moose. It could be a visual symbol of status or also an important dispenser of pheromones. Also known as dewlap.

Brain Worm an internal parasitic roundworm, fatal to moose, carried by white-tailed deer and transmitted to moose via snails or slugs. Also called meningeal worm.

Browse plant material including woody twigs, shoots and leaves.

Browser an animal that feeds on browse.

Cast to drop, as in the loss of antlers.

Cervidae the deer family, of which the moose is a member.

Chinning the placement of the bull's head across the cow's rump during the rut, possibly to transfer pheromones.

Coronet the enlarged base of the antler.

Cud regurgitated wad of partly digested plant matter, characteristic of ruminants.

Dew Claws the small horny toes on the back of a moose foot that aid in travelling across soft terrains.

Dewlap another name for the bell.

Estrus the period in which the cow ovulates and is receptive to mating advances by bulls.

False Rut the period from when the bulls first become sexually active to when the cows become receptive, usually encompassing a two- to three-week period. Also called the pre-rut.

Flemen a characteristic pose of bulls that involves an outstretched neck, open mouth and curled lips, used to enhance the analysis of female pheromones by the vomeronasal organ.

Guard Hair long body hairs that make up most of the visible coat.

Horns permanent head structures found on animals such as goats, with the outer part composed of epidermal tissue.

Jacobson's Organ a specialized sensory center in the palate of the mouth, important in analyzing sex pheromones. Also called the vomeronasal organ.

Meningeal Worm another name for the brain worm.

Mineral Licks places where moose and other ungulates lick and eat the soil to acquire minerals, especially sodium.

Moose Disease the symptoms that arise in moose due to infection by the meningeal or brain worm.

Palm the broad, flattened portion of the antlers.

Pedicles bony outgrowths of the frontal bones that give rise to the antlers.

Personal Zone the area around a bull during the rut, which he regards as his personal space.

Pheromones chemicals secreted by moose that influence the behavior of other moose.

Pre-rut another name for the false rut.

Prime Bull a bull in his peak of physical and sexual prowess, usually between the ages of six and ten years.

Proceptive Phase the stage in the estrus cycle of the cow when she allows the bull to caress and smell her vaginal area, which in turn stimulates her into the receptive phase and ovulation.

Receptive Phase the stage in the estrus cycle of the cow when ovulation and copulation occurs.

Ruminant an animal that possesses a complex stomach and regurgitates a cud for rechewing.

Rut the breeding season of the moose.

Rut Pit a shallow pit dug by a bull during the rut into which he urinates and then rolls. Also known as a wallow pit.

Senior Bull a bull past its prime.

Sex Pheromones volatile chemical substances that influence the behavior of moose during the breeding season.

Sparring usually non-violent antler jousting contests in which dominance hierarchies are sorted out.

Tapetum lucidum a special layer of reflective cells behind the retina that enhance an animal's night vision.

Teen Bull a bull that has not yet reached his prime (usually less than six years of age).

Testosterone the key hormone in bulls during the rut that activates specific behaviors and also plays a role in antler maintenance.

Thrashing the beating of a bull's antlers on shrubbery during the breeding season, possibly done to communicate the stature of the animal to other moose.

Tines the long points on a bull's antlers.

Ungulates animals that bear hooves.

Velvet the plush skin that covers the antlers during their growth.

Vomeronasal Organ another name for Jacobson's Organ.

Wallow Pit another name for rut pit.

Winter Tick an ectoparasite of moose, which is found on them during winter.

Yards areas of shelter where white-tailed deer congregate during the winter.